THIS JOURNAL
BELONG TO

NAME

_____
_____
_____
_____

ADDRESS / CONTACT

_____
_____
_____
_____

INFORMATIONS

_____
_____
_____
_____

EMERGENCY CONTACT

_____
_____
_____

ROUTE 66 ROAD TRIP JOURNAL

DATE OF THE DAY	
START PLACE	
DESTINATION	
KM TRAVELLED	COST

ACCOMPANYING PERSONS ON BOARD

LIST OF EQUIPMENT | MATERIAL

PRE-DEPARTURE CHECKLIST

START TIME   ARRIVAL TIME

WEATHER

ROAD INFORMATION

POSITIVE ASPECT	NEGATIVE ASPECT

ROUTE 66 ROAD TRIP JOURNAL

PLACES VISITED

THE ACTIVITIES CARRIED OUT

LOCAL FOOD & RESTAURANT

MEMORIES AND BEST MOMENTS

ROAD TRIP NOTE

66

66

ROUTE 66 ROAD TRIP JOURNAL

DATE OF THE DAY	
START PLACE	
DESTINATION	
KM TRAVELLED	COST

ACCOMPANYING PERSONS ON BOARD

LIST OF EQUIPMENT | MATERIAL

PRE-DEPARTURE CHECKLIST

START TIME   ARRIVAL TIME

WEATHER

ROAD INFORMATION

POSITIVE ASPECT	NEGATIVE ASPECT

ROUTE 66 ROAD TRIP JOURNAL

PLACES VISITED

THE ACTIVITIES CARRIED OUT

LOCAL FOOD & RESTAURANT

MEMORIES AND BEST MOMENTS

ROAD TRIP NOTE

ROUTE 66 ROAD TRIP JOURNAL

DATE OF THE DAY	
START PLACE	
DESTINATION	
KM TRAVELLED	COST

ACCOMPANYING PERSONS ON BOARD

LIST OF EQUIPMENT | MATERIAL

PRE-DEPARTURE CHECKLIST

START TIME   ARRIVAL TIME

WEATHER

ROAD INFORMATION

POSITIVE ASPECT	NEGATIVE ASPECT

ROUTE 66 ROAD TRIP JOURNAL

PLACES VISITED

THE ACTIVITIES CARRIED OUT

LOCAL FOOD & RESTAURANT

MEMORIES AND BEST MOMENTS

ROAD TRIP NOTE

ROUTE 66 ROAD TRIP JOURNAL

DATE OF THE DAY	
START PLACE	
DESTINATION	
KM TRAVELLED	COST

ACCOMPANYING PERSONS ON BOARD

LIST OF EQUIPMENT | MATERIAL

PRE-DEPARTURE CHECKLIST

START TIME   ARRIVAL TIME

WEATHER

ROAD INFORMATION

POSITIVE ASPECT	NEGATIVE ASPECT

ROUTE 66 ROAD TRIP JOURNAL

PLACES VISITED

_____
_____
_____
_____

THE ACTIVITIES CARRIED OUT

_____
_____
_____

LOCAL FOOD & RESTAURANT

_____
_____
_____
_____

MEMORIES AND BEST MOMENTS

_____
_____
_____
_____

ROAD TRIP NOTE

_____
_____
_____
_____
_____
_____
_____
_____
_____
_____
_____
_____
_____
_____

ROUTE 66 ROAD TRIP JOURNAL

DATE OF THE DAY	
START PLACE	
DESTINATION	
KM TRAVELLED	COST

ACCOMPANYING PERSONS ON BOARD

_____
_____
_____
_____

LIST OF EQUIPMENT | MATERIAL

_____
_____
_____
_____

PRE-DEPARTURE CHECKLIST

_____
_____
_____
_____

START TIME   ARRIVAL TIME

WEATHER

ROAD INFORMATION

POSITIVE ASPECT	NEGATIVE ASPECT

ROUTE 66 ROAD TRIP JOURNAL

PLACES VISITED

_____
_____
_____
_____

THE ACTIVITIES CARRIED OUT

_____
_____
_____
_____

LOCAL FOOD & RESTAURANT

_____
_____
_____
_____

MEMORIES AND BEST MOMENTS

_____
_____
_____
_____

ROAD TRIP NOTE

_____
_____
_____
_____
_____
_____
_____
_____
_____
_____
_____
_____
_____
_____

ROUTE 66 ROAD TRIP JOURNAL

DATE OF THE DAY			
START PLACE			
DESTINATION			
KM TRAVELLED		COST	

ACCOMPANYING PERSONS ON BOARD

LIST OF EQUIPMENT | MATERIAL

PRE-DEPARTURE CHECKLIST

START TIME   ARRIVAL TIME

WEATHER

ROAD INFORMATION

POSITIVE ASPECT	NEGATIVE ASPECT

ROUTE 66 ROAD TRIP JOURNAL

PLACES VISITED

THE ACTIVITIES CARRIED OUT

LOCAL FOOD & RESTAURANT

MEMORIES AND BEST MOMENTS

ROAD TRIP NOTE

ROUTE 66 ROAD TRIP JOURNAL

DATE OF THE DAY	
START PLACE	
DESTINATION	
KM TRAVELLED	COST

ACCOMPANYING PERSONS ON BOARD

LIST OF EQUIPMENT | MATERIAL

PRE-DEPARTURE CHECKLIST

START TIME   ARRIVAL TIME

WEATHER

ROAD INFORMATION

POSITIVE ASPECT	NEGATIVE ASPECT

ROUTE 66 ROAD TRIP JOURNAL

PLACES VISITED

THE ACTIVITIES CARRIED OUT

LOCAL FOOD & RESTAURANT

MEMORIES AND BEST MOMENTS

ROAD TRIP NOTE

ROUTE 66 ROAD TRIP JOURNAL

DATE OF THE DAY	
START PLACE	
DESTINATION	
KM TRAVELLED	COST

ACCOMPANYING PERSONS ON BOARD

LIST OF EQUIPMENT | MATERIAL

PRE-DEPARTURE CHECKLIST

START TIME   ARRIVAL TIME

WEATHER

ROAD INFORMATION

POSITIVE ASPECT	NEGATIVE ASPECT

ROUTE 66 ROAD TRIP JOURNAL

PLACES VISITED

THE ACTIVITIES CARRIED OUT

LOCAL FOOD & RESTAURANT

MEMORIES AND BEST MOMENTS

ROAD TRIP NOTE

ROUTE 66 ROAD TRIP JOURNAL

DATE OF THE DAY	
START PLACE	
DESTINATION	
KM TRAVELLED	COST

ACCOMPANYING PERSONS ON BOARD

_____
_____
_____

LIST OF EQUIPMENT | MATERIAL

_____
_____
_____

PRE-DEPARTURE CHECKLIST

_____
_____
_____
_____

START TIME   ARRIVAL TIME

WEATHER

ROAD INFORMATION

POSITIVE ASPECT	NEGATIVE ASPECT
_____	_____
_____	_____
_____	_____
_____	_____
_____	_____
_____	_____
_____	_____
_____	_____

ROUTE 66 ROAD TRIP JOURNAL

PLACES VISITED

_____
_____
_____
_____

THE ACTIVITIES CARRIED OUT

_____
_____
_____

LOCAL FOOD & RESTAURANT

_____
_____
_____
_____

MEMORIES AND BEST MOMENTS

_____
_____
_____
_____
_____

ROAD TRIP NOTE

ROUTE 66 ROAD TRIP JOURNAL

DATE OF THE DAY	
START PLACE	
DESTINATION	
KM TRAVELLED	COST

ACCOMPANYING PERSONS ON BOARD

LIST OF EQUIPMENT | MATERIAL

PRE-DEPARTURE CHECKLIST

START TIME   ARRIVAL TIME

WEATHER

ROAD INFORMATION

POSITIVE ASPECT	NEGATIVE ASPECT

ROUTE 66 ROAD TRIP JOURNAL

PLACES VISITED

_____
_____
_____
_____

THE ACTIVITIES CARRIED OUT

_____
_____
_____

LOCAL FOOD & RESTAURANT

_____
_____
_____
_____

MEMORIES AND BEST MOMENTS

_____
_____
_____
_____

ROAD TRIP NOTE

_____
_____
_____
_____
_____
_____
_____
_____
_____
_____
_____
_____
_____
_____
_____
_____

ROUTE 66 ROAD TRIP JOURNAL

DATE OF THE DAY	
START PLACE	
DESTINATION	
KM TRAVELLED	COST

ACCOMPANYING PERSONS ON BOARD

LIST OF EQUIPMENT | MATERIAL

PRE-DEPARTURE CHECKLIST

START TIME   ARRIVAL TIME

WEATHER

ROAD INFORMATION

POSITIVE ASPECT	NEGATIVE ASPECT

ROUTE 66 ROAD TRIP JOURNAL

PLACES VISITED

_____
_____
_____
_____

THE ACTIVITIES CARRIED OUT

_____
_____
_____

LOCAL FOOD & RESTAURANT

_____
_____
_____
_____

MEMORIES AND BEST MOMENTS

_____
_____
_____
_____

ROAD TRIP NOTE

_____
_____
_____
_____
_____
_____
_____
_____
_____
_____
_____
_____
_____
_____
_____
_____

ROUTE 66 ROAD TRIP JOURNAL

DATE OF THE DAY			
START PLACE			
DESTINATION			
KM TRAVELLED		COST	

ACCOMPANYING PERSONS ON BOARD

_____
_____
_____

LIST OF EQUIPMENT | MATERIAL

_____
_____
_____

PRE-DEPARTURE CHECKLIST

_____
_____
_____

START TIME   ARRIVAL TIME

WEATHER

ROAD INFORMATION

POSITIVE ASPECT	NEGATIVE ASPECT

ROUTE 66 ROAD TRIP JOURNAL

PLACES VISITED

THE ACTIVITIES CARRIED OUT

LOCAL FOOD & RESTAURANT

MEMORIES AND BEST MOMENTS

ROAD TRIP NOTE

ROUTE 66 ROAD TRIP JOURNAL

DATE OF THE DAY	
START PLACE	
DESTINATION	
KM TRAVELLED	COST

ACCOMPANYING PERSONS ON BOARD

LIST OF EQUIPMENT | MATERIAL

PRE-DEPARTURE CHECKLIST

START TIME   ARRIVAL TIME

WEATHER

ROAD INFORMATION

POSITIVE ASPECT	NEGATIVE ASPECT

ROUTE 66 ROAD TRIP JOURNAL

PLACES VISITED

_____
_____
_____
_____

THE ACTIVITIES CARRIED OUT

_____
_____
_____
_____

LOCAL FOOD & RESTAURANT

_____
_____
_____
_____

MEMORIES AND BEST MOMENTS

_____
_____
_____
_____

ROAD TRIP NOTE

_____
_____
_____
_____
_____
_____
_____
_____
_____
_____
_____
_____
_____
_____
_____
_____

ROUTE 66 ROAD TRIP JOURNAL

DATE OF THE DAY	
START PLACE	
DESTINATION	
KM TRAVELLED	COST

ACCOMPANYING PERSONS ON BOARD

_____
_____
_____

LIST OF EQUIPMENT | MATERIAL

_____
_____
_____

PRE-DEPARTURE CHECKLIST

_____
_____
_____

START TIME   ARRIVAL TIME

WEATHER

ROAD INFORMATION

POSITIVE ASPECT	NEGATIVE ASPECT

ROUTE 66 ROAD TRIP JOURNAL

PLACES VISITED

_____
_____
_____
_____

THE ACTIVITIES CARRIED OUT

_____
_____
_____
_____

LOCAL FOOD & RESTAURANT

_____
_____
_____
_____

MEMORIES AND BEST MOMENTS

_____
_____
_____
_____

ROAD TRIP NOTE

_____
_____
_____
_____
_____
_____
_____
_____
_____
_____
_____
_____

ROUTE 66 ROAD TRIP JOURNAL

DATE OF THE DAY	
START PLACE	
DESTINATION	
KM TRAVELLED	COST

ACCOMPANYING PERSONS ON BOARD

LIST OF EQUIPMENT | MATERIAL

PRE-DEPARTURE CHECKLIST

START TIME   ARRIVAL TIME

WEATHER

ROAD INFORMATION

POSITIVE ASPECT	NEGATIVE ASPECT

ROUTE 66 ROAD TRIP JOURNAL

PLACES VISITED

_____
_____
_____
_____

THE ACTIVITIES CARRIED OUT

_____
_____
_____
_____

LOCAL FOOD & RESTAURANT

_____
_____
_____
_____

MEMORIES AND BEST MOMENTS

_____
_____
_____
_____

ROAD TRIP NOTE

_____
_____
_____
_____
_____
_____
_____
_____
_____
_____
_____
_____
_____
_____

ROUTE 66 ROAD TRIP JOURNAL

DATE OF THE DAY	
START PLACE	
DESTINATION	
KM TRAVELLED	COST

ACCOMPANYING PERSONS ON BOARD

_____
_____
_____

LIST OF EQUIPMENT | MATERIAL

_____
_____
_____
_____

PRE-DEPARTURE CHECKLIST

_____
_____
_____
_____

START TIME   ARRIVAL TIME

WEATHER

ROAD INFORMATION

POSITIVE ASPECT	NEGATIVE ASPECT
_____	_____
_____	_____
_____	_____
_____	_____
_____	_____
_____	_____
_____	_____
_____	_____

ROUTE 66 ROAD TRIP JOURNAL

PLACES VISITED

_____
_____
_____

THE ACTIVITIES CARRIED OUT

_____
_____
_____

LOCAL FOOD & RESTAURANT

_____
_____
_____

MEMORIES AND BEST MOMENTS

_____
_____
_____
_____

ROAD TRIP NOTE

_____
_____
_____
_____
_____
_____
_____
_____
_____
_____
_____
_____
_____
_____

🛣️ ROUTE 66 ROAD TRIP JOURNAL 🛣️

DATE OF THE DAY	
START PLACE	
DESTINATION	
KM TRAVELLED	COST

ACCOMPANYING PERSONS ON BOARD

_____
_____
_____

LIST OF EQUIPMENT | MATERIAL

_____
_____
_____

PRE-DEPARTURE CHECKLIST

_____
_____
_____

START TIME   ARRIVAL TIME

WEATHER

ROAD INFORMATION

POSITIVE ASPECT	NEGATIVE ASPECT
_____	_____
_____	_____
_____	_____
_____	_____
_____	_____
_____	_____
_____	_____
_____	_____

ROUTE 66 ROAD TRIP JOURNAL

PLACES VISITED

_____
_____
_____
_____

THE ACTIVITIES CARRIED OUT

_____
_____
_____
_____

LOCAL FOOD & RESTAURANT

_____
_____
_____
_____

MEMORIES AND BEST MOMENTS

_____
_____
_____
_____

ROAD TRIP NOTE

ROUTE 66 ROAD TRIP JOURNAL

DATE OF THE DAY	
START PLACE	
DESTINATION	
KM TRAVELLED	COST

ACCOMPANYING PERSONS ON BOARD

_____
_____
_____
_____

LIST OF EQUIPMENT | MATERIAL

_____
_____
_____
_____

PRE-DEPARTURE CHECKLIST

_____
_____
_____
_____

START TIME   ARRIVAL TIME

WEATHER

ROAD INFORMATION

POSITIVE ASPECT	NEGATIVE ASPECT

ROUTE 66 ROAD TRIP JOURNAL

PLACES VISITED

_____
_____
_____
_____
_____

THE ACTIVITIES CARRIED OUT

_____
_____
_____
_____

LOCAL FOOD & RESTAURANT

_____
_____
_____
_____
_____

MEMORIES AND BEST MOMENTS

_____
_____
_____
_____
_____

ROAD TRIP NOTE

_____
_____
_____
_____
_____
_____
_____
_____
_____
_____
_____
_____
_____
_____
_____
_____
_____

ROUTE 66 ROAD TRIP JOURNAL

DATE OF THE DAY	
START PLACE	
DESTINATION	
KM TRAVELLED	COST

ACCOMPANYING PERSONS ON BOARD

LIST OF EQUIPMENT | MATERIAL

PRE-DEPARTURE CHECKLIST

START TIME   ARRIVAL TIME

WEATHER

ROAD INFORMATION

POSITIVE ASPECT	NEGATIVE ASPECT

ROUTE 66 ROAD TRIP JOURNAL

PLACES VISITED

_____
_____
_____
_____

THE ACTIVITIES CARRIED OUT

_____
_____
_____
_____

LOCAL FOOD & RESTAURANT

_____
_____
_____
_____

MEMORIES AND BEST MOMENTS

_____
_____
_____
_____

ROAD TRIP NOTE

_____
_____
_____
_____
_____
_____
_____
_____
_____
_____
_____
_____

ROUTE 66 ROAD TRIP JOURNAL

DATE OF THE DAY			
START PLACE			
DESTINATION			
KM TRAVELLED		COST	

ACCOMPANYING PERSONS ON BOARD

LIST OF EQUIPMENT | MATERIAL

PRE-DEPARTURE CHECKLIST

START TIME   ARRIVAL TIME

WEATHER

ROAD INFORMATION

POSITIVE ASPECT	NEGATIVE ASPECT

ROUTE 66 ROAD TRIP JOURNAL

PLACES VISITED

_____
_____
_____
_____

THE ACTIVITIES CARRIED OUT

_____
_____
_____

LOCAL FOOD & RESTAURANT

_____
_____
_____
_____

MEMORIES AND BEST MOMENTS

_____
_____
_____
_____
_____

ROAD TRIP NOTE

_____
_____
_____
_____
_____
_____
_____
_____
_____
_____
_____
_____
_____
_____
_____
_____

ROUTE 66 ROAD TRIP JOURNAL

DATE OF THE DAY	
START PLACE	
DESTINATION	
KM TRAVELLED	COST

ACCOMPANYING PERSONS ON BOARD

_____
_____
_____
_____

LIST OF EQUIPMENT | MATERIAL

_____
_____
_____
_____

PRE-DEPARTURE CHECKLIST

_____
_____
_____
_____

START TIME   ARRIVAL TIME

WEATHER

ROAD INFORMATION

POSITIVE ASPECT	NEGATIVE ASPECT

ROUTE 66 ROAD TRIP JOURNAL

PLACES VISITED

_____
_____
_____
_____

THE ACTIVITIES CARRIED OUT

_____
_____
_____

LOCAL FOOD & RESTAURANT

_____
_____
_____
_____

MEMORIES AND BEST MOMENTS

_____
_____
_____
_____

ROAD TRIP NOTE

_____
_____
_____
_____
_____
_____
_____
_____
_____
_____
_____
_____
_____
_____
_____
_____

ROUTE 66 ROAD TRIP JOURNAL

DATE OF THE DAY	
START PLACE	
DESTINATION	
KM TRAVELLED	COST

ACCOMPANYING PERSONS ON BOARD

_____
_____
_____
_____

LIST OF EQUIPMENT | MATERIAL

_____
_____
_____
_____

PRE-DEPARTURE CHECKLIST

_____
_____
_____
_____

START TIME   ARRIVAL TIME

WEATHER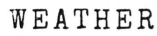

ROAD INFORMATION

POSITIVE ASPECT	NEGATIVE ASPECT

ROUTE 66 ROAD TRIP JOURNAL

PLACES VISITED

_____
_____
_____
_____

THE ACTIVITIES CARRIED OUT

_____
_____
_____
_____

LOCAL FOOD & RESTAURANT

_____
_____
_____
_____

MEMORIES AND BEST MOMENTS

_____
_____
_____
_____

ROAD TRIP NOTE

_____
_____
_____
_____
_____
_____
_____
_____
_____
_____
_____
_____

ROUTE 66 ROAD TRIP JOURNAL

DATE OF THE DAY			
START PLACE			
DESTINATION			
KM TRAVELLED		COST	

ACCOMPANYING PERSONS ON BOARD

_____
_____
_____

LIST OF EQUIPMENT | MATERIAL

_____
_____
_____
_____

PRE-DEPARTURE CHECKLIST

_____
_____
_____
_____

START TIME   ARRIVAL TIME

WEATHER

ROAD INFORMATION

POSITIVE ASPECT	NEGATIVE ASPECT

ROUTE 66 ROAD TRIP JOURNAL

PLACES VISITED

_____
_____
_____
_____

THE ACTIVITIES CARRIED OUT

_____
_____
_____

LOCAL FOOD & RESTAURANT

_____
_____
_____
_____

MEMORIES AND BEST MOMENTS

_____
_____
_____
_____

ROAD TRIP NOTE

⬡ROUTE 66⬡ ROUTE 66 ROAD TRIP JOURNAL ⬡ROUTE 66⬡

DATE OF THE DAY		
START PLACE		
DESTINATION		
KM TRAVELLED		COST

ACCOMPANYING PERSONS ON BOARD

_____
_____
_____

LIST OF EQUIPMENT | MATERIAL

_____
_____
_____

PRE-DEPARTURE CHECKLIST

_____
_____
_____
_____

START TIME   ARRIVAL TIME

WEATHER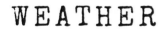

ROAD INFORMATION

POSITIVE ASPECT	NEGATIVE ASPECT
_____	_____
_____	_____
_____	_____
_____	_____
_____	_____
_____	_____
_____	_____
_____	_____

ROUTE 66 ROAD TRIP JOURNAL

PLACES VISITED

_____
_____
_____
_____

THE ACTIVITIES CARRIED OUT

_____
_____
_____
_____
_____

LOCAL FOOD & RESTAURANT

_____
_____
_____
_____
_____

MEMORIES AND BEST MOMENTS

_____
_____
_____
_____
_____

ROAD TRIP NOTE

_____
_____
_____
_____
_____
_____
_____
_____
_____
_____
_____
_____
_____
_____
_____
_____
_____
_____

ROUTE 66 ROAD TRIP JOURNAL

DATE OF THE DAY			
START PLACE			
DESTINATION			
KM TRAVELLED		COST	

ACCOMPANYING PERSONS ON BOARD

LIST OF EQUIPMENT | MATERIAL

PRE-DEPARTURE CHECKLIST

START TIME   ARRIVAL TIME

WEATHER

ROAD INFORMATION

POSITIVE ASPECT	NEGATIVE ASPECT

ROUTE 66 ROAD TRIP JOURNAL

PLACES VISITED

THE ACTIVITIES CARRIED OUT

LOCAL FOOD & RESTAURANT

MEMORIES AND BEST MOMENTS

ROAD TRIP NOTE

ROUTE 66 ROAD TRIP JOURNAL

DATE OF THE DAY	
START PLACE	
DESTINATION	
KM TRAVELLED	COST

ACCOMPANYING PERSONS ON BOARD

_____
_____
_____

LIST OF EQUIPMENT | MATERIAL

_____
_____
_____

PRE-DEPARTURE CHECKLIST

_____
_____
_____

START TIME   ARRIVAL TIME

WEATHER

ROAD INFORMATION

POSITIVE ASPECT	NEGATIVE ASPECT

ROUTE 66 ROAD TRIP JOURNAL

PLACES VISITED

_____
_____
_____

THE ACTIVITIES CARRIED OUT

_____
_____
_____

LOCAL FOOD & RESTAURANT

_____
_____
_____
_____

MEMORIES AND BEST MOMENTS

_____
_____
_____
_____

ROAD TRIP NOTE

_____
_____
_____
_____
_____
_____
_____
_____
_____
_____
_____
_____
_____
_____

ROUTE 66 ROAD TRIP JOURNAL

DATE OF THE DAY	
START PLACE	
DESTINATION	
KM TRAVELLED	COST

ACCOMPANYING PERSONS ON BOARD

_____
_____
_____

LIST OF EQUIPMENT | MATERIAL

_____
_____
_____

PRE-DEPARTURE CHECKLIST

_____
_____
_____
_____

START TIME   ARRIVAL TIME

WEATHER

ROAD INFORMATION

POSITIVE ASPECT	NEGATIVE ASPECT

ROUTE 66 ROAD TRIP JOURNAL

PLACES VISITED

THE ACTIVITIES CARRIED OUT

LOCAL FOOD & RESTAURANT

MEMORIES AND BEST MOMENTS

ROAD TRIP NOTE

ROUTE 66 ROAD TRIP JOURNAL

DATE OF THE DAY	
START PLACE	
DESTINATION	
KM TRAVELLED	COST

ACCOMPANYING PERSONS ON BOARD

LIST OF EQUIPMENT | MATERIAL

PRE-DEPARTURE CHECKLIST

START TIME   ARRIVAL TIME

WEATHER

ROAD INFORMATION

POSITIVE ASPECT	NEGATIVE ASPECT

ROUTE 66 ROAD TRIP JOURNAL

PLACES VISITED

_____
_____
_____

THE ACTIVITIES CARRIED OUT

_____
_____
_____

LOCAL FOOD & RESTAURANT

_____
_____
_____

MEMORIES AND BEST MOMENTS

_____
_____
_____
_____

ROAD TRIP NOTE

_____
_____
_____
_____
_____
_____
_____
_____
_____
_____
_____
_____
_____
_____
_____
_____

ROUTE 66 ROAD TRIP JOURNAL

DATE OF THE DAY			
START PLACE			
DESTINATION			
KM TRAVELLED		COST	

ACCOMPANYING PERSONS ON BOARD

_____
_____
_____

LIST OF EQUIPMENT | MATERIAL

_____
_____
_____

PRE-DEPARTURE CHECKLIST

_____
_____
_____

START TIME   ARRIVAL TIME

WEATHER

ROAD INFORMATION

POSITIVE ASPECT	NEGATIVE ASPECT
_____	_____
_____	_____
_____	_____
_____	_____
_____	_____
_____	_____
_____	_____
_____	_____

ROUTE 66 ROAD TRIP JOURNAL

PLACES VISITED

THE ACTIVITIES CARRIED OUT

LOCAL FOOD & RESTAURANT

MEMORIES AND BEST MOMENTS

ROAD TRIP NOTE

ROUTE 66 ROAD TRIP JOURNAL

DATE OF THE DAY	
START PLACE	
DESTINATION	
KM TRAVELLED	COST

ACCOMPANYING PERSONS ON BOARD

LIST OF EQUIPMENT | MATERIAL

PRE-DEPARTURE CHECKLIST

START TIME   ARRIVAL TIME

WEATHER

ROAD INFORMATION

POSITIVE ASPECT	NEGATIVE ASPECT

ROUTE 66 ROAD TRIP JOURNAL

PLACES VISITED

_____
_____
_____
_____

THE ACTIVITIES CARRIED OUT

_____
_____
_____
_____

LOCAL FOOD & RESTAURANT

_____
_____
_____
_____

MEMORIES AND BEST MOMENTS

_____
_____
_____
_____

ROAD TRIP NOTE

_____
_____
_____
_____
_____
_____
_____
_____
_____
_____
_____
_____
_____
_____
_____

ROUTE 66 ROAD TRIP JOURNAL

DATE OF THE DAY	
START PLACE	
DESTINATION	
KM TRAVELLED	COST

ACCOMPANYING PERSONS ON BOARD

_____
_____
_____

LIST OF EQUIPMENT | MATERIAL

_____
_____
_____

PRE-DEPARTURE CHECKLIST

_____
_____
_____

START TIME   ARRIVAL TIME

WEATHER

ROAD INFORMATION

POSITIVE ASPECT	NEGATIVE ASPECT
_____	_____
_____	_____
_____	_____
_____	_____
_____	_____
_____	_____
_____	_____

PLACES VISITED

_____
_____
_____
_____

THE ACTIVITIES CARRIED OUT

_____
_____
_____

LOCAL FOOD & RESTAURANT

_____
_____
_____

MEMORIES AND BEST MOMENTS

_____
_____
_____
_____

ROAD TRIP NOTE

_____
_____
_____
_____
_____
_____
_____
_____
_____
_____
_____

DATE OF THE DAY	
START PLACE	
DESTINATION	
KM TRAVELLED	COST

ACCOMPANYING PERSONS ON BOARD

_____
_____
_____

LIST OF EQUIPMENT | MATERIAL

_____
_____
_____

PRE-DEPARTURE CHECKLIST

_____
_____
_____
_____

START TIME   ARRIVAL TIME

WEATHER

ROAD INFORMATION

POSITIVE ASPECT	NEGATIVE ASPECT

ROUTE 66 ROAD TRIP JOURNAL

PLACES VISITED

THE ACTIVITIES CARRIED OUT

LOCAL FOOD & RESTAURANT

MEMORIES AND BEST MOMENTS

ROAD TRIP NOTE

ROUTE 66 ROAD TRIP JOURNAL

DATE OF THE DAY	
START PLACE	
DESTINATION	
KM TRAVELLED	COST

ACCOMPANYING PERSONS ON BOARD

_____
_____
_____

LIST OF EQUIPMENT | MATERIAL

_____
_____
_____
_____

PRE-DEPARTURE CHECKLIST

_____
_____
_____
_____

START TIME   ARRIVAL TIME

WEATHER

ROAD INFORMATION

POSITIVE ASPECT	NEGATIVE ASPECT

ROUTE 66 ROAD TRIP JOURNAL

PLACES VISITED

_____
_____
_____
_____

THE ACTIVITIES CARRIED OUT

_____
_____
_____

LOCAL FOOD & RESTAURANT

_____
_____
_____
_____

MEMORIES AND BEST MOMENTS

_____
_____
_____
_____

ROAD TRIP NOTE

ROUTE 66 ROAD TRIP JOURNAL

DATE OF THE DAY		
START PLACE		
DESTINATION		
KM TRAVELLED		COST

ACCOMPANYING PERSONS ON BOARD

LIST OF EQUIPMENT | MATERIAL

PRE-DEPARTURE CHECKLIST

START TIME   ARRIVAL TIME

WEATHER

ROAD INFORMATION

POSITIVE ASPECT	NEGATIVE ASPECT

ROUTE 66 ROAD TRIP JOURNAL

PLACES VISITED

_____
_____
_____
_____

THE ACTIVITIES CARRIED OUT

_____
_____
_____

LOCAL FOOD & RESTAURANT

_____
_____
_____
_____

MEMORIES AND BEST MOMENTS

_____
_____
_____
_____

ROAD TRIP NOTE

_____
_____
_____
_____
_____
_____
_____
_____
_____
_____
_____
_____
_____
_____

ROUTE 66 ROAD TRIP JOURNAL

DATE OF THE DAY	
START PLACE	
DESTINATION	
KM TRAVELLED	COST

ACCOMPANYING PERSONS ON BOARD

_____
_____
_____
_____

LIST OF EQUIPMENT | MATERIAL

_____
_____
_____
_____

PRE-DEPARTURE CHECKLIST

_____
_____
_____
_____

START TIME   ARRIVAL TIME

WEATHER

ROAD INFORMATION

POSITIVE ASPECT	NEGATIVE ASPECT
_____	_____
_____	_____
_____	_____
_____	_____
_____	_____
_____	_____
_____	_____
_____	_____

ROUTE 66 ROAD TRIP JOURNAL

PLACES VISITED

_____
_____
_____
_____

THE ACTIVITIES CARRIED OUT

_____
_____
_____
_____

LOCAL FOOD & RESTAURANT

_____
_____
_____
_____

MEMORIES AND BEST MOMENTS

_____
_____
_____
_____

ROAD TRIP NOTE

_____
_____
_____
_____
_____
_____
_____
_____
_____
_____
_____
_____
_____

ROUTE 66 ROAD TRIP JOURNAL

DATE OF THE DAY	
START PLACE	
DESTINATION	
KM TRAVELLED	COST

ACCOMPANYING PERSONS ON BOARD

_____
_____
_____

LIST OF EQUIPMENT | MATERIAL

_____
_____
_____

PRE-DEPARTURE CHECKLIST

_____
_____
_____

START TIME   ARRIVAL TIME

WEATHER

ROAD INFORMATION

POSITIVE ASPECT	NEGATIVE ASPECT

ROUTE 66 ROAD TRIP JOURNAL

PLACES VISITED

_____
_____
_____
_____

THE ACTIVITIES CARRIED OUT

_____
_____
_____
_____

LOCAL FOOD & RESTAURANT

_____
_____
_____
_____

MEMORIES AND BEST MOMENTS

_____
_____
_____
_____
_____

ROAD TRIP NOTE

ROUTE 66 ROAD TRIP JOURNAL

DATE OF THE DAY	
START PLACE	
DESTINATION	
KM TRAVELLED	COST

ACCOMPANYING PERSONS ON BOARD

_____
_____
_____

LIST OF EQUIPMENT | MATERIAL

_____
_____
_____

PRE-DEPARTURE CHECKLIST

_____
_____
_____

START TIME   ARRIVAL TIME

WEATHER

ROAD INFORMATION

POSITIVE ASPECT	NEGATIVE ASPECT
_____	_____
_____	_____
_____	_____
_____	_____
_____	_____
_____	_____
_____	_____

ROUTE 66 ROAD TRIP JOURNAL

PLACES VISITED

_____
_____
_____
_____

THE ACTIVITIES CARRIED OUT

_____
_____
_____
_____

LOCAL FOOD & RESTAURANT

_____
_____
_____
_____

MEMORIES AND BEST MOMENTS

_____
_____
_____
_____

ROAD TRIP NOTE

_____
_____
_____
_____
_____
_____
_____
_____
_____
_____
_____
_____
_____
_____

ROUTE 66 ROAD TRIP JOURNAL

DATE OF THE DAY	
START PLACE	
DESTINATION	
KM TRAVELLED	COST

ACCOMPANYING PERSONS ON BOARD

_____
_____
_____

LIST OF EQUIPMENT | MATERIAL

_____
_____
_____

PRE-DEPARTURE CHECKLIST

_____
_____
_____
_____

START TIME   ARRIVAL TIME

WEATHER

ROAD INFORMATION

POSITIVE ASPECT	NEGATIVE ASPECT
_____	_____
_____	_____
_____	_____
_____	_____
_____	_____
_____	_____
_____	_____
_____	_____
_____	_____

PLACES VISITED

_____
_____
_____
_____

THE ACTIVITIES CARRIED OUT

_____
_____
_____

LOCAL FOOD & RESTAURANT

_____
_____
_____

MEMORIES AND BEST MOMENTS

_____
_____
_____
_____

ROAD TRIP NOTE

_____
_____
_____
_____
_____
_____
_____
_____
_____
_____
_____
_____
_____

ROUTE 66 ROAD TRIP JOURNAL

DATE OF THE DAY	
START PLACE	
DESTINATION	
KM TRAVELLED	COST

ACCOMPANYING PERSONS ON BOARD

_____
_____
_____

LIST OF EQUIPMENT | MATERIAL

_____
_____
_____
_____

PRE-DEPARTURE CHECKLIST

_____
_____
_____
_____

START TIME   ARRIVAL TIME

WEATHER

ROAD INFORMATION

POSITIVE ASPECT	NEGATIVE ASPECT

ROUTE 66 ROAD TRIP JOURNAL

PLACES VISITED

_____
_____
_____
_____

THE ACTIVITIES CARRIED OUT

_____
_____
_____
_____

LOCAL FOOD & RESTAURANT

_____
_____
_____
_____

MEMORIES AND BEST MOMENTS

_____
_____
_____
_____
_____

ROAD TRIP NOTE

_____
_____
_____
_____
_____
_____
_____
_____
_____
_____
_____
_____
_____
_____
_____
_____
_____

ROUTE 66 ROAD TRIP JOURNAL

DATE OF THE DAY			
START PLACE			
DESTINATION			
KM TRAVELLED		COST	

ACCOMPANYING PERSONS ON BOARD

_____
_____
_____

LIST OF EQUIPMENT | MATERIAL

_____
_____
_____

PRE-DEPARTURE CHECKLIST

_____
_____
_____

START TIME   ARRIVAL TIME

WEATHER

ROAD INFORMATION

POSITIVE ASPECT	NEGATIVE ASPECT

ROUTE 66 ROAD TRIP JOURNAL

PLACES VISITED

_____
_____
_____
_____

THE ACTIVITIES CARRIED OUT

_____
_____
_____
_____

LOCAL FOOD & RESTAURANT

_____
_____
_____
_____

MEMORIES AND BEST MOMENTS

_____
_____
_____
_____

ROAD TRIP NOTE

_____
_____
_____
_____
_____
_____
_____
_____
_____
_____
_____
_____

ROUTE 66 ROAD TRIP JOURNAL

DATE OF THE DAY			
START PLACE			
DESTINATION			
KM TRAVELLED		COST	

ACCOMPANYING PERSONS ON BOARD

LIST OF EQUIPMENT | MATERIAL

PRE-DEPARTURE CHECKLIST

START TIME   ARRIVAL TIME

WEATHER

ROAD INFORMATION

POSITIVE ASPECT	NEGATIVE ASPECT

ROUTE 66 ROAD TRIP JOURNAL

PLACES VISITED

THE ACTIVITIES CARRIED OUT

LOCAL FOOD & RESTAURANT

MEMORIES AND BEST MOMENTS

ROAD TRIP NOTE

ROUTE 66 ROAD TRIP JOURNAL

DATE OF THE DAY		
START PLACE		
DESTINATION		
KM TRAVELLED		COST

ACCOMPANYING PERSONS ON BOARD

_____
_____
_____
_____

LIST OF EQUIPMENT | MATERIAL

_____
_____
_____
_____

PRE-DEPARTURE CHECKLIST

_____
_____
_____
_____

START TIME   ARRIVAL TIME

WEATHER

ROAD INFORMATION

POSITIVE ASPECT	NEGATIVE ASPECT
_____	_____
_____	_____
_____	_____
_____	_____
_____	_____
_____	_____
_____	_____
_____	_____

ROUTE 66 ROAD TRIP JOURNAL

PLACES VISITED

THE ACTIVITIES CARRIED OUT

LOCAL FOOD & RESTAURANT

MEMORIES AND BEST MOMENTS

ROAD TRIP NOTE

ROUTE 66 ROAD TRIP JOURNAL

DATE OF THE DAY			
START PLACE			
DESTINATION			
KM TRAVELLED		COST	

ACCOMPANYING PERSONS ON BOARD

_____
_____
_____
_____

LIST OF EQUIPMENT | MATERIAL

_____
_____
_____
_____

PRE-DEPARTURE CHECKLIST

_____
_____
_____
_____

START TIME   ARRIVAL TIME

WEATHER

ROAD INFORMATION

POSITIVE ASPECT	NEGATIVE ASPECT

ROUTE 66 ROAD TRIP JOURNAL

PLACES VISITED

THE ACTIVITIES CARRIED OUT

LOCAL FOOD & RESTAURANT

MEMORIES AND BEST MOMENTS

ROAD TRIP NOTE

66

66

ROUTE 66 ROAD TRIP JOURNAL

DATE OF THE DAY	
START PLACE	
DESTINATION	
KM TRAVELLED	COST

ACCOMPANYING PERSONS ON BOARD

_____
_____
_____

LIST OF EQUIPMENT | MATERIAL

_____
_____
_____

PRE-DEPARTURE CHECKLIST

_____
_____
_____

START TIME   ARRIVAL TIME

WEATHER

ROAD INFORMATION

POSITIVE ASPECT	NEGATIVE ASPECT
_____	_____
_____	_____
_____	_____
_____	_____
_____	_____
_____	_____
_____	_____

ROUTE 66 ROAD TRIP JOURNAL

PLACES VISITED

_____
_____
_____
_____

THE ACTIVITIES CARRIED OUT

_____
_____
_____
_____

LOCAL FOOD & RESTAURANT

_____
_____
_____
_____

MEMORIES AND BEST MOMENTS

_____
_____
_____
_____

ROAD TRIP NOTE

_____
_____
_____
_____
_____
_____
_____
_____
_____
_____
_____
_____
_____
_____

ROUTE 66 ROAD TRIP JOURNAL

DATE OF THE DAY	
START PLACE	
DESTINATION	
KM TRAVELLED	COST

ACCOMPANYING PERSONS ON BOARD

_____
_____
_____

LIST OF EQUIPMENT | MATERIAL

_____
_____
_____
_____

PRE-DEPARTURE CHECKLIST

_____
_____
_____
_____

START TIME   ARRIVAL TIME

WEATHER

ROAD INFORMATION

POSITIVE ASPECT	NEGATIVE ASPECT
_____	_____
_____	_____
_____	_____
_____	_____
_____	_____
_____	_____
_____	_____
_____	_____
_____	_____

ROUTE 66 ROAD TRIP JOURNAL

PLACES VISITED

_____
_____
_____
_____

THE ACTIVITIES CARRIED OUT

_____
_____
_____
_____

LOCAL FOOD & RESTAURANT

_____
_____
_____
_____

MEMORIES AND BEST MOMENTS

_____
_____
_____
_____

ROAD TRIP NOTE

_____
_____
_____
_____
_____
_____
_____
_____
_____
_____
_____
_____
_____

ROUTE 66 ROAD TRIP JOURNAL

DATE OF THE DAY	
START PLACE	
DESTINATION	
KM TRAVELLED	COST

ACCOMPANYING PERSONS ON BOARD

LIST OF EQUIPMENT | MATERIAL

PRE-DEPARTURE CHECKLIST

START TIME   ARRIVAL TIME

WEATHER

ROAD INFORMATION

POSITIVE ASPECT	NEGATIVE ASPECT

ROUTE 66 ROAD TRIP JOURNAL

PLACES VISITED

_____
_____
_____
_____

THE ACTIVITIES CARRIED OUT

_____
_____
_____
_____

LOCAL FOOD & RESTAURANT

_____
_____
_____
_____

MEMORIES AND BEST MOMENTS

_____
_____
_____
_____

ROAD TRIP NOTE

_____
_____
_____
_____
_____
_____
_____
_____
_____
_____
_____
_____
_____
_____

ROUTE 66 ROAD TRIP JOURNAL

DATE OF THE DAY	
START PLACE	
DESTINATION	
KM TRAVELLED	COST

ACCOMPANYING PERSONS ON BOARD

_____
_____
_____
_____

LIST OF EQUIPMENT | MATERIAL

_____
_____
_____
_____

PRE-DEPARTURE CHECKLIST

_____
_____
_____
_____

START TIME   ARRIVAL TIME

WEATHER

ROAD INFORMATION

POSITIVE ASPECT	NEGATIVE ASPECT
_____	_____
_____	_____
_____	_____
_____	_____
_____	_____
_____	_____
_____	_____
_____	_____

ROUTE 66 ROAD TRIP JOURNAL

PLACES VISITED

_____
_____
_____
_____
_____

THE ACTIVITIES CARRIED OUT

_____
_____
_____
_____

LOCAL FOOD & RESTAURANT

_____
_____
_____
_____

MEMORIES AND BEST MOMENTS

_____
_____
_____
_____

ROAD TRIP NOTE

ROUTE 66 ROAD TRIP JOURNAL

DATE OF THE DAY			
START PLACE			
DESTINATION			
KM TRAVELLED		COST	

ACCOMPANYING PERSONS ON BOARD

_____
_____
_____

LIST OF EQUIPMENT | MATERIAL

_____
_____
_____

PRE-DEPARTURE CHECKLIST

_____
_____
_____

START TIME   ARRIVAL TIME

WEATHER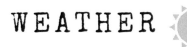

ROAD INFORMATION

POSITIVE ASPECT	NEGATIVE ASPECT

ROUTE 66 ROAD TRIP JOURNAL

PLACES VISITED

_____
_____
_____
_____

THE ACTIVITIES CARRIED OUT

_____
_____
_____

LOCAL FOOD & RESTAURANT

_____
_____
_____
_____

MEMORIES AND BEST MOMENTS

_____
_____
_____
_____

ROAD TRIP NOTE

ROUTE 66 ROAD TRIP JOURNAL

DATE OF THE DAY	
START PLACE	
DESTINATION	
KM TRAVELLED	COST

ACCOMPANYING PERSONS ON BOARD

LIST OF EQUIPMENT | MATERIAL

PRE-DEPARTURE CHECKLIST

START TIME   ARRIVAL TIME

WEATHER

ROAD INFORMATION

POSITIVE ASPECT	NEGATIVE ASPECT

ROUTE 66 ROAD TRIP JOURNAL

PLACES VISITED

_____
_____
_____
_____

THE ACTIVITIES CARRIED OUT

_____
_____
_____
_____

LOCAL FOOD & RESTAURANT

_____
_____
_____
_____

MEMORIES AND BEST MOMENTS

_____
_____
_____
_____

ROAD TRIP NOTE

ROUTE 66 ROAD TRIP JOURNAL

DATE OF THE DAY	
START PLACE	
DESTINATION	
KM TRAVELLED	COST

ACCOMPANYING PERSONS ON BOARD

_____
_____
_____

LIST OF EQUIPMENT | MATERIAL

_____
_____
_____

PRE-DEPARTURE CHECKLIST

_____
_____
_____

START TIME   ARRIVAL TIME

WEATHER

ROAD INFORMATION

POSITIVE ASPECT	NEGATIVE ASPECT

ROUTE 66 ROAD TRIP JOURNAL

PLACES VISITED

_____
_____
_____
_____

THE ACTIVITIES CARRIED OUT

_____
_____
_____

LOCAL FOOD & RESTAURANT

_____
_____
_____
_____

MEMORIES AND BEST MOMENTS

_____
_____
_____
_____

ROAD TRIP NOTE

_____
_____
_____
_____
_____
_____
_____
_____
_____
_____
_____
_____

Made in United States
North Haven, CT
22 May 2022

19426873R00057